# KETO Λ

# COOKBOOK

## The Ultimate Guide to Quick and Delicious Low Carb Recipes for Busy People

**SUSAN VICTORIA**

# TABLE OF CONTENT

# INTRODUCTION

In today's fast-paced world, finding the time to prepare healthy and delicious meals can often be a challenge. That's where the convenience and simplicity of mug recipes come to the rescue. Imagine whipping up a mouthwatering keto dish in a matter of minutes, all within the confines of a single mug. Sounds incredible, right? Well, get ready to embark on a culinary journey that combines the principles of the ketogenic diet with the convenience of single-serve cooking.

This book is a celebration of the ketogenic lifestyle and the incredible possibilities that can be achieved with just a mug and a microwave. Whether you're a busy professional, a student on-the-go, or simply someone looking for quick and satisfying low-carb meals, this collection of keto mug recipes is here to revolutionize your kitchen experience.

Within the pages of this book, you'll discover an array of tantalizing breakfasts, hearty soups, delectable main courses, scrumptious desserts, and everything in between – all created to fit seamlessly into your ketogenic journey. Each recipe has been carefully crafted to provide a balance of healthy fats, moderate protein, and low-carbohydrate options that will keep you on track with your dietary goals.

But this book is more than just a collection of recipes. It's a comprehensive guide that will equip you with the knowledge and confidence to master the art of mug cooking. You'll learn about essential ingredients and tools, helpful tips for success, and troubleshooting common issues that may arise during the cooking process. With this knowledge in hand, you'll be well-prepared to create the perfect mug dish every time.

Whether you're a kitchen novice or an experienced cook, you'll find the instructions clear, concise, and easy to follow. Each recipe is designed with simplicity in mind, making them accessible to all skill levels. So, don your apron, grab your favorite mug, and get ready to embark on a culinary adventure that will revolutionize the way you approach keto cooking.

As you flip through the pages of this book, you'll be greeted with vibrant photographs that showcase the mouthwatering creations that await you. These visual delights will inspire you to unleash your creativity in the kitchen, experimenting with flavors, textures, and unique combinations to suit your personal taste.

Whether you're craving a hearty breakfast to start your day, a comforting soup to warm your soul, or a decadent dessert to satisfy your sweet tooth, the recipes in this book will fulfill your desires without compromising your commitment to a healthy lifestyle.

So, get ready to discover the magic of keto mug recipes and elevate your culinary experience to new heights. Embrace the simplicity, embrace the flavor, and embrace the joy of single-serve cooking. Let this book be your trusted companion on your ketogenic journey, as you savor the convenience and delight of keto mug recipes that will nourish your body and tantalize your taste buds.

# CHAPTER ONE

## What is the ketogenic diet?

The keto diet, short for ketogenic diet, is a low-carbohydrate, high-fat diet that has gained popularity for its potential health benefits and weight loss effects. The primary goal of the keto diet is to shift the body's metabolism from relying on carbohydrates for energy to using fats as its primary fuel source. By drastically reducing carbohydrate intake and increasing fat consumption, the body enters a state called ketosis.

In a standard diet, carbohydrates are the primary source of energy, and they are broken down into glucose, which is used by the body for fuel. However, when carbohydrate intake is significantly reduced, the body turns to an alternative fuel source: fat. In ketosis, the liver breaks down fat into molecules called ketones, which serve as an energy source for the body, including the brain.

**Here are some key characteristics of the ketogenic diet:**

**Low Carbohydrate Intake**: The keto diet typically restricts carbohydrate intake to around 20-50 grams per day, or about 5-10% of total calories. This limitation is designed to deplete the body's glycogen stores and promote the use of fat as the primary fuel source.

**High Fat Intake**: The keto diet emphasizes consuming a higher proportion of healthy fats, typically making up around 70-75% of total calories. Good sources of fat include avocados, nuts and seeds, olive oil, coconut oil, and fatty cuts of meat.

**Moderate Protein Intake**: Protein intake is moderate in the keto diet, usually comprising around 20-25% of total calories. Sources of protein can include meat, poultry, fish, eggs, and plant-based protein sources like tofu and tempeh.

**Ketosis:** By severely limiting carbohydrate intake, the body enters a state of ketosis, where it primarily burns fat for energy. This can lead to weight loss and increased fat burning.

# Benefits of the keto diet

The keto diet has been associated with several potential benefits. Here are some of the commonly reported advantages:

**1. Weight Loss**: The keto diet is often effective for weight loss due to its ability to promote fat burning. When carbohydrate intake is limited, the body relies on stored fat as its primary source of energy, leading to weight loss over time.

**2. Appetite Control**: The high-fat and moderate-protein content of the keto diet can help increase feelings of fullness and satiety. This can result in reduced cravings and a decreased appetite, making it easier to adhere to a calorie deficit and manage portion sizes.

**3. Blood Sugar Control**: The keto diet can be beneficial for individuals with diabetes or insulin resistance. By minimizing carbohydrate intake, the keto diet helps regulate blood sugar levels and reduce insulin spikes. This can improve insulin sensitivity and may have a positive impact on managing blood sugar levels.

**4. Improved Mental Focus**: Some people report increased mental clarity and improved cognitive function while following a keto diet. The brain can efficiently use ketones as an alternative fuel source, which may lead to enhanced mental performance.

**5. Increased Energy Levels**: Once the body adapts to using fat as its primary fuel source, many individuals experience sustained energy levels throughout the day. They may avoid the energy crashes often associated with high-carbohydrate meals.

**6. Reduced Inflammation**: The keto diet has been suggested to have anti-inflammatory effects. By reducing carbohydrate intake, which can contribute to inflammation, some individuals may experience a decrease in inflammatory markers.

**7. Potential Health Benefits**: The keto diet has shown promise in certain health conditions, including epilepsy, metabolic syndrome, polycystic ovary syndrome (PCOS), and some neurological disorders. However, it's important to note that individual results may vary, and the keto diet should be implemented under the guidance of a healthcare professional.

# CHAPTER TWO

## How to use mugs for keto cooking

Using mugs for keto cooking is a convenient and efficient way to prepare single-serve keto-friendly meals and snacks. Here are some tips on how to use mugs for keto cooking:

**1. Mug Selection**: Choose microwave-safe mugs that can withstand high temperatures. Avoid mugs with metallic accents or materials that are not safe for microwave use.

**2. Portion Control**: Mugs provide built-in portion control, making it easier to adhere to your desired serving size. This is especially helpful when following a specific macronutrient ratio on the keto diet.

**3. Ingredient Preparation**: Prepare your ingredients ahead of time to ensure a smooth cooking process. Chop vegetables, shred cheese, and measure out spices and seasonings before starting.

**4. Mixing and Combining Ingredients**: Mugs are great for mixing ingredients together. Use a fork or spoon to combine wet and dry ingredients thoroughly. Ensure there are no lumps or uneven distribution of ingredients.

**5. Cooking Times and Power Levels**: Microwave cooking times can vary, so it's essential to monitor your food closely to avoid overcooking. Start with the suggested cooking time in the recipe, but be prepared to adjust based on your microwave's power level.

**6. Stirring and Checking Progress**: During the cooking process, pause and stir the contents of the mug to ensure even cooking. Check the progress by inserting a toothpick or small knife into the center of the food to see if it comes out clean or if further cooking is required.

**7. Letting it Rest**: After cooking, allow the mug to rest for a minute or two. The food will continue to cook slightly, and the heat will distribute evenly throughout.

**8. Garnishing and Serving**: Add toppings or garnishes to enhance the flavor and presentation of your keto mug dish. Sprinkle herbs, grated cheese, or a dollop of sour cream on top, depending on the recipe.

**9. Experiment with Recipes**: Explore a variety of keto mug recipes to keep your meals interesting. From mug cakes to soups and omelettes, there are numerous possibilities for keto-friendly meals in a mug.

**10. Safety Precautions**: Always handle hot mugs with oven mitts or kitchen towels to prevent burns. Be cautious when removing the mug from the microwave as it can be very hot.

## Essential tools for mug cooking

When it comes to mug cooking for the keto diet, a few essential tools can make the process easier and more efficient. Here are some tools you may find helpful:

**1. Microwave-Safe Mugs:** Choose microwave-safe mugs that are suitable for high-temperature cooking. Look for mugs made of ceramic, glass, or microwave-safe plastic. Avoid mugs with metallic accents or materials that are not safe for microwave use.

**2. Measuring Spoons and Cups**: Accurate measurements are crucial for successful mug cooking. Have a set of measuring spoons and cups on hand to measure ingredients precisely, especially when following keto recipes that require specific ratios and portions.

**3. Mixing Utensils**: Use a fork or spoon for mixing and combining ingredients in the mug. Silicone spatulas or small whisk-like utensils can also come in handy for thoroughly blending wet and dry ingredients.

**4. Cutting Board and Knife**: A small cutting board and a sharp knife are essential for prepping ingredients, such as chopping vegetables or cutting small pieces of cheese or meat. Ensure the knife is suitable for the task and handle it safely.

**5. Microwave Oven**: Mug cooking heavily relies on the microwave oven for quick and convenient cooking. Ensure you have access to a microwave oven with adjustable power levels and a turntable for even heating.

**6. Oven Mitts or Kitchen Towels**: Microwaved mugs can become very hot, so it's important to use oven mitts or kitchen towels when handling them. This will help protect your hands from burns.

**7. Toothpick or Small Knife**: Keep toothpicks or a small knife handy for checking the doneness of your mug dishes. Insert them into the center of the food to see if it comes out clean or if further cooking is required.

**8. Microwave Cover or Microwave-Safe Plate:** To prevent messy splatters inside your microwave, consider using a microwave cover or a microwave-safe plate to cover the mug while cooking. This helps contain any spills or splatters and keeps your microwave clean.

**9. Timer or Clock:** Accurate timing is crucial for mug cooking. Use a timer or keep an eye on the clock to ensure you don't overcook or undercook your keto mug dishes.

These essential tools will help you prepare and cook keto-friendly meals efficiently in mugs. As you experiment with mug cooking, you may discover additional tools or gadgets that suit your preferences and make the process even more enjoyable.

## Common Ingredients for keto mug recipes

When it comes to keto mug recipes, there are various ingredients you can use to create delicious and low-carb dishes. Here are some common ingredients for keto mug recipes:

**1. Almond Flour**: Almond flour is a popular low-carb alternative to traditional wheat flour. It adds a nutty flavor and a tender texture to mug cakes, muffins, and breads.

**2. Coconut Flour**: Coconut flour is another keto-friendly flour option. It absorbs more liquid than almond flour, so you'll typically use less of it in recipes. It provides a light and fluffy texture to mug cakes and breads.

**3. Eggs**: Eggs are a staple ingredient in many keto mug recipes as they add structure, moisture, and protein. They are often used as a binding agent in mug cakes, omelettes, and muffins.

**4. Butter or Coconut Oil**: These healthy fats are commonly used in keto cooking. They add richness, flavor, and moisture to mug recipes. Choose grass-fed butter or unrefined coconut oil for added nutritional benefits.

**5. Unsweetened Almond Milk or Coconut Milk**: These dairy-free milk alternatives are low in carbs and can be used to moisten mug cakes and other recipes. Look for unsweetened versions to keep the carb count low.

**6. Sweeteners**: Keto-friendly sweeteners like stevia, erythritol, or monk fruit sweetener can be used to add sweetness to mug desserts without spiking blood sugar levels. Use them sparingly, as they are much sweeter than sugar.

**7. Cocoa Powder:** Unsweetened cocoa powder adds a rich chocolate flavor to keto mug cakes and hot chocolate recipes. Look for a high-quality, unsweetened variety without added sugars.

**8. Cream Cheese:** Cream cheese is a versatile ingredient that adds creaminess and flavor to both sweet and savory mug recipes. It works well in mug cakes, dips, and mug cheesecakes.

**9. Low-Carb Vegetables**: Incorporate low-carb vegetables like spinach, zucchini, broccoli, or cauliflower into savory mug recipes. They add texture, nutrients, and bulk to your meals.

**10. Cheese**: Cheese is a great source of flavor and adds richness to keto mug recipes. Use shredded cheese or cream cheese in savory mug dishes like soups, omelettes, and mug pizzas.

**11. Spices and Seasonings**: Enhance the taste of your keto mug recipes with herbs, spices, and seasonings such as cinnamon, vanilla extract, garlic powder, onion powder, chili flakes, or Italian seasoning.

**12. Nuts and Seeds:** Chopped nuts, such as almonds or walnuts, can add crunch and healthy fats to mug recipes. Chia seeds and flaxseeds can also be used to provide texture and added nutrition.

# CHAPTER THREE

## KETO MUG RECIPES

### 1. Keto Mug Bread:

**Ingredients:**
- 3 tablespoons almond flour
- 1 tablespoon ground flaxseed
- ¼ teaspoon baking powder
- Pinch of salt
- 1 large egg
- 1 tablespoon melted butter or coconut oil

**Preparation:**

1. In a microwave-safe mug, whisk together the almond flour, ground flaxseed, baking powder, and salt.

2. Add the egg and melted butter or coconut oil to the mug. Mix well until all ingredients are combined.

3. Microwave on high for about 90 seconds, or until the bread is cooked through and springs back when touched.

4. Allow the mug bread to cool slightly before slicing and enjoying.

**Average Preparation Time**: 5 minutes

## 2. Keto Mug Cake (Chocolate):

**Ingredients**:
- 3 tablespoons almond flour
- 1 tablespoon unsweetened cocoa powder
- 1 tablespoon low-carb sweetener (such as stevia or erythritol)
- ¼ teaspoon baking powder
- Pinch of salt
- 1 large egg
- 2 tablespoons almond milk (or any low-carb milk)
- 1 tablespoon melted butter or coconut oil
- Optional: sugar-free chocolate chips or chopped nuts for topping

**Preparation:**

1. In a microwave-safe mug, whisk together the almond flour, cocoa powder, sweetener, baking powder, and salt.

2. Add the egg, almond milk, and melted butter or coconut oil to the mug. Mix well until smooth and combined.

3. Microwave on high for about 60-90 seconds, or until the cake is set in the middle.

4. Allow the mug cake to cool for a few minutes before adding optional toppings and enjoying.

**Average Preparation Time**: 5 minutes

## 3. Keto Mug Omelette:

### Ingredients:

- 2 large eggs
- 2 tablespoons heavy cream or unsweetened almond milk
- 2 tablespoons shredded cheese
- 2 tablespoons diced vegetables (such as bell peppers, onions, or spinach)
- Salt and pepper to taste
- Optional: cooked bacon or sausage, chopped

**Preparation:**

1. In a microwave-safe mug, whisk together the eggs and heavy cream or almond milk.

2. Stir in the shredded cheese, diced vegetables, and optional cooked bacon or sausage. Season with salt and pepper.

3. Microwave on high for about 2-3 minutes, stirring halfway through, until the eggs are set.

4. Let the mug omelette cool for a minute before serving.

**Average Preparation Time**: 5 minutes

# 4. Keto Mug Brownie:

## Ingredients:
- 2 tablespoons almond flour
- 1 tablespoon unsweetened cocoa powder
- 1 tablespoon low-carb sweetener (such as stevia or erythritol)
- Pinch of salt
- 1 tablespoon melted butter or coconut oil
- 1 tablespoon almond milk (or any low-carb milk)
- Optional: sugar-free chocolate chips or chopped nuts for topping

## Preparation:

1. In a microwave-safe mug, whisk together the almond flour, cocoa powder, sweetener, and salt.

2. Add the melted butter or coconut oil and almond milk to the mug. Mix well until smooth and combined.

3. Microwave on high for about 60-90 seconds, or until the brownie is cooked but still fudgy in the center.

4. Let the mug brownie cool for a minute, add optional toppings, and enjoy.

**Average Preparation Time**: 5 minutes

## 5. Keto Mug Pizza:

### Ingredients:

- 3 tablespoons almond flour
- 1 tablespoon coconut flour
- ¼ teaspoon baking powder
¼ teaspoon Italian seasoning
- Pinch of salt
- 1 large egg
- 1 tablespoon olive oil
- 1 tablespoon low-carb pizza sauce
- Shredded cheese
- Toppings of your choice (such as sliced pepperoni, bell peppers, or mushrooms)

## Preparation:

1. In a microwave-safe mug, whisk together the almond flour, coconut flour, baking powder, Italian seasoning, and salt.
2. Add the egg and olive oil to the mug. Mix well until a batter forms.
3. Spread the low-carb pizza sauce on top of the batter in the mug. Add a layer of shredded cheese and your desired toppings.
4. Microwave on high for about 90 seconds, or until the cheese is melted and bubbly.
5. Let the mug pizza cool for a minute before slicing and enjoying.

**Average Preparation Time**: 10 minutes

# 6. Keto Mug Muffin (Blueberry):

**Ingredients**:
- 3 tablespoons almond flour
- 1 tablespoon coconut flour
- 1 tablespoon low-carb sweetener (such as stevia or erythritol)
- ¼ teaspoon baking powder
- Pinch of salt
- 1 large egg
- 1 tablespoon melted butter or coconut oil
- 2 tablespoons unsweetened almond milk (or any low-carb milk)
- ¼ teaspoon vanilla extract
- 2 tablespoons fresh or frozen blueberries

**Preparation:**

1. In a microwave-safe mug, whisk together the almond flour, coconut flour, sweetener, baking powder, and salt.

2. Add the egg, melted butter or coconut oil, almond milk, and vanilla extract to the mug. Mix well until smooth and combined.

3. Gently fold in the blueberries.

4. Microwave on high for about 90 seconds, or until the muffin is cooked through.

5. Allow the muffin to cool for a few minutes before enjoying.

**Average Preparation Time**: 5 minutes

## 7. Keto Mug Pancake:

### Ingredients:
- 2 tablespoons almond flour
- 1 tablespoon coconut flour
- 1 tablespoon low-carb sweetener (such as stevia or erythritol)
- ¼ teaspoon baking powder
- Pinch of salt
- 1 large egg
- 2 tablespoons unsweetened almond milk (or any low-carb milk)
- ½ teaspoon vanilla extract
- Optional: sugar-free syrup or berries for topping

### Preparation:

1. In a microwave-safe mug, whisk together the almond flour, coconut flour, sweetener, baking powder, and salt.

2. Add the egg, almond milk, and vanilla extract to the mug. Mix well until smooth and combined.

3. Microwave on high for about 90 seconds, or until the pancake is cooked and set.

4. Allow the pancake to cool for a minute before adding optional toppings and enjoying.

**Average Preparation Time**: 5 minutes

# 8. Keto Mug Quiche:

## Ingredients:
- 2 large eggs
- 2 tablespoons heavy cream or unsweetened almond milk
- 2 tablespoons shredded cheese
- 2 tablespoons diced vegetables (such as spinach, mushrooms, or onions)
- Salt and pepper to taste
- Optional: cooked bacon or sausage, chopped

## Preparation:

1. In a microwave-safe mug, whisk together the eggs and heavy cream or almond milk.

2. Stir in the shredded cheese, diced vegetables, and optional cooked bacon or sausage. Season with salt and pepper.

3. Microwave on high for about 2-3 minutes, stirring halfway through, until the eggs are set.

4. Let the mug quiche cool for a minute before serving.

**Average Preparation Time**: 5 minutes

# 9. Keto Mug Cinnamon Roll:

## Ingredients:
- 3 tablespoons almond flour
- 1 tablespoon coconut flour
- 1 tablespoon low-carb sweetener (such as stevia or erythritol)
- ½ teaspoon ground cinnamon
- ¼ teaspoon baking powder
- Pinch of salt
- 1 large egg
- 1 tablespoon melted butter or coconut oil
- Optional: cream cheese frosting (made with cream cheese, sweetener, and a splash of vanilla extract)

## Preparation:

1. In a microwave-safe mug, whisk together the almond flour, coconut flour, sweetener, cinnamon, baking powder, and salt.

2. Add the egg and melted butter or coconut oil to the mug. Mix well until smooth and combined.

3. Microwave on high for about 60-90 seconds, or until the cinnamon roll is cooked through.

4. Allow the cinnamon roll to cool for a minute before drizzling with optional cream cheese frosting (if desired).

**Average Preparation Time**: 5 minutes

# 10. Keto Mug Lasagna:

## Ingredients:
- ¼ cup ground beef or ground turkey
- 2 tablespoons low-carb marinara sauce
- 2 tablespoons ricotta cheese
- 2 tablespoons shredded mozzarella cheese
- ¼ teaspoon Italian seasoning
- Salt and pepper to taste
- Optional: chopped fresh basil for garnish

## Preparation:

1. In a microwave-safe mug, cook the ground beef or turkey until browned and cooked through.

2. Drain any excess fat from the mug and add the marinara sauce, ricotta cheese, shredded mozzarella cheese, Italian seasoning, salt, and pepper. Mix well.

3. Microwave on high for about 1-2 minutes, or until the cheese is melted and bubbly.

4. Let the lasagna cool for a minute before garnishing with optional fresh basil and serving.

**Average Preparation Time**: 10 minutes

# 11. Keto Mug Scramble (Eggs, Bacon, and Cheese):

**Ingredients:**
- 2 large eggs
- 2 tablespoons heavy cream or unsweetened almond milk
- 2 slices cooked bacon, crumbled
- 2 tablespoons shredded cheese
- Salt and pepper to taste
- Optional: chopped green onions or fresh herbs for garnish

**Preparation:**

1. In a microwave-safe mug, whisk together the eggs and heavy cream or almond milk.

2. Stir in the crumbled bacon and shredded cheese. Season with salt and pepper.

3. Microwave on high for about 2-3 minutes, stirring halfway through, until the eggs are set.

4. Sprinkle with optional chopped green onions or fresh herbs before serving.

**Average Preparation Time:** 5 minutes

# 12. Keto Mug Pumpkin Spice Cake:

**Ingredients:**
- 3 tablespoons almond flour
- 1 tablespoon coconut flour
- 1 tablespoon low-carb sweetener (such as stevia or erythritol)
- ¼ teaspoon baking powder
- ¼ teaspoon pumpkin pie spice
- Pinch of salt
- 1 large egg
- 1 tablespoon melted butter or coconut oil
- 1 tablespoon unsweetened almond milk (or any low-carb milk)
- 1 tablespoon pumpkin puree
- Optional: whipped cream or cream cheese frosting for topping

**Preparation:**

1. In a microwave-safe mug, whisk together the almond flour, coconut flour, sweetener, baking powder, pumpkin pie spice, and salt.
2. Add the egg, melted butter or coconut oil, almond milk, and pumpkin puree to the mug. Mix well until smooth and combined.
3. Microwave on high for about 60-90 seconds, or until the cake is cooked through.
4. Let the pumpkin spice cake cool for a minute before adding optional whipped cream or cream cheese frosting (if desired).

**Average Preparation Time**: 5 minutes

## 13. Keto Mug Mac and Cheese:

### Ingredients:
- ¼ cup cauliflower florets, cooked and mashed
- 2 tablespoons heavy cream or unsweetened almond milk
- 2 tablespoons shredded cheese (such as cheddar or mozzarella)
- 1 tablespoon grated Parmesan cheese
- Pinch of garlic powder
- Pinch of onion powder
- Pinch of paprika
- Salt and pepper to taste

**Preparation:**

1. In a microwave-safe mug, combine the mashed cauliflower, heavy cream or almond milk, shredded cheese, grated Parmesan cheese, garlic powder, onion powder, paprika, salt, and pepper.

2. Microwave on high for about 1-2 minutes, stirring halfway through, until the cheese is melted and the mixture is heated through.

3. Let the mac and cheese cool for a minute before enjoying.

**Average Preparation Time:** 5 minutes

# 14. Keto Mug Chocolate Chip Cookie:

## Ingredients:

- 1 tablespoon butter, melted
- 1 tablespoon low-carb sweetener (such as stevia or erythritol)
- 1 tablespoon almond flour
- 1 tablespoon coconut flour
- Pinch of baking powder
- Pinch of salt
- 1 tablespoon sugar-free chocolate chips

## Preparation:

1. In a microwave-safe mug, combine the melted butter, sweetener, almond flour, coconut flour, baking powder, and salt.

2. Mix well until a dough forms. Fold in the sugar-free chocolate chips.

3. Microwave on high for about 60-90 seconds, or until the cookie is cooked but still soft in the center.

4. Allow the cookie to cool for a minute before enjoying.

**Average Preparation Time**: 5 minutes

## 15. Keto Mug Breakfast Burrito:

**Ingredients:**

- 2 large eggs

- 2 tablespoons heavy cream or unsweetened almond milk

- 2 tablespoons shredded cheese

- 2 tablespoons diced cooked bacon or sausage

- 1 tablespoon diced bell peppers

- Salt and pepper to taste

- Optional: salsa or avocado slices for topping

**Preparation:**

1. In a microwave-safe mug, whisk together the eggs and heavy cream or almond milk.

2. Stir in the shredded cheese, diced bacon or sausage, and diced bell peppers. Season with salt and pepper.

3. Microwave on high for about 2-3 minutes, stirring halfway through, until the eggs are set.

4. Top with optional salsa or avocado slices before serving.

**Average Preparation Time**: 5 minutes

# 16. Keto Mug Cheesecake:

## Ingredients:
- 2 tablespoons cream cheese, softened
- 1 tablespoon heavy cream or unsweetened almond milk
- 1 tablespoon low-carb sweetener (such as stevia or erythritol)
- ¼ teaspoon vanilla extract
- Pinch of lemon zest (optional)
- Optional: whipped cream or sugar-free fruit preserves for topping

## Preparation:

1. In a microwave-safe mug, combine the cream cheese, heavy cream or almond milk, sweetener, vanilla extract, and lemon zest (if using).

2. Mix well until smooth and creamy.

3. Microwave on high for about 60-90 seconds, or until the cheesecake is set.

4. Let the cheesecake cool for a minute before adding optional whipped cream or sugar-free fruit preserves.

**Average Preparation Time:** 5 minutes

## 17. Keto Mug Lemon Poppy Seed Muffin:

Ingredients:
- 3 tablespoons almond flour
- 1 tablespoon coconut flour
- 1 tablespoon low-carb sweetener (such as stevia or erythritol)
- ¼ teaspoon baking powder
- Pinch of salt
- 1 large egg
- 1 tablespoon melted butter or coconut oil
- 1 tablespoon lemon juice
- ½ teaspoon lemon zest
- ½ teaspoon poppy seeds

**Preparation**:

1. In a microwave-safe mug, whisk together the almond flour, coconut flour, sweetener, baking powder, and salt.

2. Add the egg, melted butter or coconut oil, lemon juice, lemon zest, and poppy seeds to the mug. Mix well until smooth and combined.

3. Microwave on high for about 60-90 seconds, or until the muffin is cooked through.

4. Allow the muffin to cool for a few minutes before enjoying.

**Average Preparation Time**: 5 minutes

# 18. Keto Mug Taco Bowl:

**Ingredients:**
- ¼ cup ground beef or ground turkey
- 1 tablespoon taco seasoning
- 2 tablespoons shredded cheese
- 2 tablespoons diced tomatoes
- 1 tablespoon diced onions
- 1 tablespoon diced bell peppers
- Optional: sour cream or guacamole for topping

**Preparation:**

1. In a microwave-safe mug, cook the ground beef or turkey until browned and cooked through.

2. Drain any excess fat from the mug and stir in the taco seasoning.

3. Top with shredded cheese, diced tomatoes, onions, and bell peppers.

4. Microwave on high for about 1-2 minutes, or until the cheese is melted and the ingredients are heated through.

5. Garnish with optional sour cream or guacamole before serving.

**Average Preparation Time:** 10 minutes

## 19. Keto Mug Peanut Butter Cookie:

### Ingredients:

- 1 tablespoon unsweetened peanut butter
- 1 tablespoon almond flour
- 1 tablespoon low-carb sweetener (such as stevia or erythritol)
- 1 tablespoon beaten egg
- Pinch of salt

**Preparation:**

1. In a microwave-safe mug, combine the peanut butter, almond flour, sweetener, beaten egg, and salt.

2. Mix well until a dough forms.

3. Microwave on high for about 60-90 seconds, or until the cookie is cooked but still soft in the center.

4. Allow the cookie to cool for a minute before enjoying.

**Average Preparation Time:** 5 minutes

# 20. Keto Mug Chicken Pot Pie:

## Ingredients:
- ¼ cup cooked chicken, diced
- 2 tablespoons diced vegetables (such as carrots, peas, or green beans)
- 2 tablespoons heavy cream or unsweetened almond milk
- 1 tablespoon shredded cheese
- Pinch of garlic powder
- Pinch of onion powder
- Pinch of dried thyme
- Pinch of dried rosemary
- Salt and pepper to taste

## Preparation:

1. In a microwave-safe mug, combine the diced chicken, diced vegetables, heavy cream or almond milk, shredded cheese, garlic powder, onion powder, dried thyme, dried rosemary, salt, and pepper.

2. Microwave on high for about 1-2 minutes, stirring halfway through, until the ingredients are heated through.

3. Let the chicken pot pie cool for a minute before serving.

**Average Preparation Time**: 5 minutes

## 21. Keto Mug French Toast:

**Ingredients:**
- 1 large egg
- 2 tablespoons heavy cream or unsweetened almond milk
- 1 tablespoon melted butter
- 1 tablespoon low-carb sweetener (such as stevia or erythritol)
- ½ teaspoon vanilla extract
- Pinch of cinnamon
- 1 slice of low-carb bread, cubed

**Preparation:**

1. In a microwave-safe mug, whisk together the egg, heavy cream or almond milk, melted butter, sweetener, vanilla extract, and cinnamon.

2. Add the cubed low-carb bread to the mug and press it down to soak up the mixture.

3. Microwave on high for about 1-2 minutes, or until the French toast is cooked through and slightly crispy.

4. Let the French toast cool for a minute before serving. Optional: Serve with sugar-free syrup or berries.

**Average Preparation Time**: 5 minutes

## 22. Keto Mug Buffalo Chicken Dip:

### Ingredients:

- 2 tablespoons cooked shredded chicken
- 2 tablespoons cream cheese, softened
- 1 tablespoon hot sauce (such as Frank's RedHot)
- 1 tablespoon sour cream
- 1 tablespoon shredded cheddar cheese
- 1 tablespoon diced celery (optional)
- Pinch of garlic powder
- Pinch of onion powder

### Preparation:

1. In a microwave-safe mug, combine the shredded chicken, cream cheese, hot sauce, sour cream, shredded cheddar cheese, diced celery (if using), garlic powder, and onion powder.

2. Mix well until all ingredients are combined.

3. Microwave on high for about 1-2 minutes, or until the dip is heated through and the cheese is melted.

4. Let the buffalo chicken dip cool for a minute before enjoying. Optional: Serve with celery sticks or low-carb crackers.

**Average Preparation Time**: 5 minutes

## 23. Keto Mug Biscuit:

### Ingredients:

- 3 tablespoons almond flour

- 1 tablespoon melted butter

- 1 tablespoon sour cream

- ¼ teaspoon baking powder

- Pinch of salt

**Preparation:**

1. In a microwave-safe mug, combine the almond flour, melted butter, sour cream, baking powder, and salt.

2. Mix well until a dough forms.

3. Microwave on high for about 60-90 seconds, or until the biscuit is cooked through.

4. Let the biscuit cool for a minute before serving. Optional: Slice and toast for a crispier texture.

**Average Preparation Time**: 5 minutes

# 24. Keto Mug Berry Cobbler:

## Ingredients:
- ¼ cup mixed berries (such as strawberries, blueberries, and raspberries)
- 2 tablespoons almond flour
- 1 tablespoon melted butter
- 1 tablespoon low-carb sweetener (such as stevia or erythritol)
- Pinch of cinnamon
- Pinch of salt
- Optional: whipped cream or sugar-free ice cream for topping

## Preparation:

1. In a microwave-safe mug, combine the mixed berries, almond flour, melted butter, sweetener, cinnamon, and salt.

2. Mix well until the berries are coated and the ingredients are combined.

3. Microwave on high for about 60-90 seconds, or until the cobbler is bubbling and the topping is cooked through.

4. Let the berry cobbler cool for a minute before adding optional whipped cream or sugar-free ice cream.

**Average Preparation Time**: 5 minutes

## 25. Keto Mug Eggplant Parmesan:

**Ingredients:**
- ¼ cup diced eggplant
- 2 tablespoons low-carb marinara sauce
2 tablespoons shredded mozzarella cheese
- 1 tablespoon grated Parmesan cheese
- Pinch of garlic powder
- Pinch of dried basil
- Pinch of dried oregano
- Salt and pepper to taste

**Preparation:**

1. In a microwave-safe mug, layer the diced eggplant, marinara sauce, shredded mozzarella cheese, grated Parmesan cheese, garlic powder, dried basil, dried oregano, salt, and pepper.

2. Repeat the layers until the mug is almost full, finishing with a layer of cheese on top.

3. Microwave on high for about 2-3 minutes, or until the cheese is melted and bubbly.

4. Let the eggplant Parmesan cool for a minute before serving.

**Average Preparation Time**: 5 minutes

# 26. Keto Mug S'mores Cake:

**Ingredients**:
- 2 tablespoons almond flour
- 1 tablespoon cocoa powder
- 1 tablespoon low-carb sweetener (such as stevia or erythritol)
- ¼ teaspoon baking powder
- Pinch of salt
- 1 tablespoon melted butter
- 1 tablespoon unsweetened almond milk
- 1 tablespoon sugar-free chocolate chips
- 1 tablespoon crushed low-carb graham crackers
- 1 tablespoon mini sugar-free marshmallows

**Preparation:**

1. In a microwave-safe mug, whisk together the almond flour, cocoa powder, sweetener, baking powder, and salt.

2. Add the melted butter and almond milk to the mug. Mix well until smooth and combined.

3. Stir in the sugar-free chocolate chips, crushed graham crackers, and mini marshmallows.

4. Microwave on high for about 60-90 seconds, or until the cake is cooked but still soft in the center.

5. Allow the S'mores cake to cool for a minute before enjoying.

**Average Preparation Time**: 5 minutes

# 27. Keto Mug Spinach and Feta Quiche:

## Ingredients:
- 2 tablespoons chopped fresh spinach
- 2 tablespoons crumbled feta cheese
- 2 tablespoons heavy cream or unsweetened almond milk
- 1 large egg
- Pinch of garlic powder
- Pinch of onion powder
- Salt and pepper to taste

## Preparation:

1. In a microwave-safe mug, layer the chopped spinach and crumbled feta cheese.

2. In a separate bowl, whisk together the heavy cream or almond milk, egg, garlic powder, onion powder, salt, and pepper.

3. Pour the egg mixture over the spinach and feta in the mug.

4. Microwave on high for about 2-3 minutes, or until the quiche is set and cooked through.

5. Let the spinach and feta quiche cool for a minute before serving.

**Average Preparation Time**: 5 minutes

## 28. Keto Mug Chocolate Lava Cake:

### Ingredients:
- 1 tablespoon unsweetened cocoa powder
- 1 tablespoon almond flour
- 1 tablespoon low-carb sweetener (such as stevia or erythritol)
- ¼ teaspoon baking powder
- Pinch of salt
- 1 tablespoon melted butter
- 1 tablespoon unsweetened almond milk
- 1 teaspoon sugar-free chocolate chips

### Preparation:

1. In a microwave-safe mug, whisk together the cocoa powder, almond flour, sweetener, baking powder, and salt.

2. Add the melted butter and almond milk to the mug. Mix well until smooth and combined.

3. Stir in the sugar-free chocolate chips.

4. Microwave on high for about 60-90 seconds, or until the cake is cooked but still has a molten center.

5. Allow the chocolate lava cake to cool for a minute before enjoying. Optional: Serve with whipped cream or sugar-free ice cream.

**Average Preparation Time:** 5 minutes

## 29. Keto Mug Chicken Alfredo:

### Ingredients:
- ¼ cup cooked diced chicken
- 2 tablespoons heavy cream
- 1 tablespoon grated Parmesan cheese
- 1 tablespoon cream cheese
- 1 tablespoon unsalted butter
- Pinch of garlic powder
- Pinch of dried parsley
- Salt and pepper to taste

**Preparation:**

1. In a microwave-safe mug, combine the diced chicken, heavy cream, grated Parmesan cheese, cream cheese, butter, garlic powder, dried parsley, salt, and pepper.

2. Microwave on high for about 1-2 minutes, stirring halfway through, until the sauce is creamy and the chicken is heated through.

3. Let the chicken Alfredo cool for a minute before serving.

**Average Preparation Time**: 5 minutes

# 30. Keto Mug Pecan Pie:

**Ingredients:**
- 2 tablespoons almond flour
- 1 tablespoon low-carb sweetener (such as stevia or erythritol)
- 1 tablespoon melted butter
- 1 tablespoon sugar-free maple syrup
- 1 tablespoon chopped pecans
- Pinch of cinnamon
- Pinch of salt

**Preparation:**

1. In a microwave-safe mug, combine the almond flour, sweetener, melted butter, sugar-free maple syrup, chopped pecans, cinnamon, and salt.

2. Mix well until the ingredients are combined.

3. Microwave on high for about 60-90 seconds, or until the pecan pie is cooked through.

4. Let the pecan pie cool for a minute before serving. Optional: Top with whipped cream or a drizzle of additional sugar-free maple syrup.

**Average Preparation Time**: 5 minutes

## 31. Keto Mug Taco Salad:

**Ingredients:**
- 2 tablespoons ground beef or turkey
- 1 tablespoon taco seasoning
- 2 tablespoons shredded lettuce
- 1 tablespoon diced tomatoes
- 1 tablespoon diced avocado
- 1 tablespoon shredded cheddar cheese
- 1 tablespoon sour cream
- Optional toppings: sliced olives, diced onions, chopped cilantro

**Preparation:**

1. In a microwave-safe mug, cook the ground beef or turkey until browned.

2. Drain any excess fat and stir in the taco seasoning.

3. Layer the shredded lettuce, diced tomatoes, diced avocado, shredded cheddar cheese, and cooked ground meat in the mug.

4. Microwave on high for about 1-2 minutes, or until the cheese is melted and the ingredients are heated through.

5. Top with sour cream and optional toppings.

6. Let the taco salad cool for a minute before enjoying.

**Average Preparation Time**: 5 minutes

# 32. Keto Mug Vanilla Cake:

## Ingredients:
- 3 tablespoons almond flour
- 1 tablespoon coconut flour
- 1 tablespoon low-carb sweetener (such as stevia or erythritol)
- ¼ teaspoon baking powder
- Pinch of salt
- 1 large egg
- 1 tablespoon melted butter
- 1 tablespoon unsweetened almond milk
- ½ teaspoon vanilla extract

## Preparation:

1. In a microwave-safe mug, whisk together the almond flour, coconut flour, sweetener, baking powder, and salt.

2. Add the egg, melted butter, almond milk, and vanilla extract to the mug. Mix well until smooth and combined.

3. Microwave on high for about 60-90 seconds, or until the cake is cooked but still moist.

4. Let the vanilla cake cool for a minute before enjoying.

**Average Preparation Time**: 5 minutes

## 33. Keto Mug Broccoli and Cheddar Soup:

### Ingredients:
- ½ cup chopped broccoli florets
- 2 tablespoons heavy cream
- 2 tablespoons shredded cheddar cheese
- 1 tablespoon cream cheese
- Pinch of garlic powder
- Pinch of onion powder
- Salt and pepper to taste

### Preparation:

1. In a microwave-safe mug, combine the chopped broccoli florets, heavy cream, shredded cheddar cheese, cream cheese, garlic powder, onion powder, salt, and pepper.

2. Microwave on high for about 2-3 minutes, or until the broccoli is tender and the cheese is melted.

3. Stir the soup well to combine all the ingredients.

4. Let the broccoli and cheddar soup cool for a minute before serving.

**Average Preparation Time:** 5 minutes

### 34. Keto Mug Coconut Flour Pancake:

**Ingredients:**
- 2 tablespoons coconut flour
- 1 tablespoon low-carb sweetener (such as stevia or erythritol)
- ¼ teaspoon baking powder
- Pinch of salt
- 2 tablespoons unsweetened almond milk
- 1 tablespoon melted butter
- 1 large egg

Preparation:

1. In a microwave-safe mug, whisk together the coconut flour, sweetener, baking powder, and salt.

2. Add the almond milk, melted butter, and egg to the mug. Mix well until smooth and combined.

3. Microwave on high for about 60-90 seconds, or until the pancake is cooked through and fluffy.

4. Let the coconut flour pancake cool for a minute before enjoying. Optional: Serve with sugar-free syrup or fresh berries.

**Average Preparation Time**: 5 minutes

## 35. Keto Mug Beef Stroganoff:

### Ingredients:
- 2 tablespoons sliced mushrooms
- 2 tablespoons diced onion
- 2 tablespoons diced cooked beef
- 2 tablespoons sour cream
- 2 tablespoons beef broth
- Pinch of garlic powder
- Pinch of dried thyme
- Salt and pepper to taste

**Preparation:**

1. In a microwave-safe mug, combine the sliced mushrooms, diced onion, diced cooked beef, sour cream, beef broth, garlic powder, dried thyme, salt, and pepper.

2. Microwave on high for about 2-3 minutes, or until the mushrooms are tender and the mixture is heated through.

3. Stir the beef stroganoff well to combine all the ingredients.

4. Let it cool for a minute before enjoying.

**Average Preparation Time**: 5 minutes

# 36. Keto Mug Strawberry Shortcake:

## Ingredients:
- 3 tablespoons almond flour
- 1 tablespoon coconut flour
- 1 tablespoon low-carb sweetener (such as stevia or erythritol)
- ¼ teaspoon baking powder
- Pinch of salt
- 1 tablespoon melted butter
- 1 tablespoon unsweetened almond milk
- ¼ teaspoon vanilla extract
- 2-3 sliced strawberries
- Whipped cream for topping (optional)

## Preparation:

1. In a microwave-safe mug, whisk together the almond flour, coconut flour, sweetener, baking powder, and salt.

2. Add the melted butter, almond milk, and vanilla extract to the mug. Mix well until smooth and combined.

3. Microwave on high for about 60-90 seconds, or until the cake is cooked through and slightly firm.

4. Let the strawberry shortcake cool for a minute before topping it with sliced strawberries and optional whipped cream.

**Average Preparation Time:** 5 minutes

## 37. Keto Mug Chili:

### Ingredients:
- 2 tablespoons ground beef or turkey
- 2 tablespoons diced tomatoes
- 1 tablespoon diced bell pepper
- 1 tablespoon diced onion
- 1 teaspoon chili powder
- ¼ teaspoon cumin
- Pinch of garlic powder
- Pinch of onion powder
- Salt and pepper to taste

**Preparation:**

1. In a microwave-safe mug, cook the ground beef or turkey until browned.

2. Drain any excess fat and add the diced tomatoes, diced bell pepper, diced onion, chili powder, cumin, garlic powder, onion powder, salt, and pepper to the mug.

3. Microwave on high for about 2-3 minutes, or until the chili is heated through.

4. Stir the chili well to combine all the ingredients.

5. Let it cool for a minute before enjoying.

**Average Preparation Time**: 5 minutes

# 38. Keto Mug Zucchini Bread:

**Ingredients:**
- 3 tablespoons almond flour
- 1 tablespoon coconut flour
- 1 tablespoon low-carb sweetener (such as stevia or erythritol)
- ¼ teaspoon baking powder
- Pinch of salt
- 1 tablespoon melted butter
- 1 tablespoon unsweetened almond milk
- 2 tablespoons grated zucchini
- ¼ teaspoon vanilla extract
- Pinch of cinnamon (optional)

**Preparation:**

1. In a microwave-safe mug, whisk together the almond flour, coconut flour, sweetener, baking powder, and salt.

2. Add the melted butter, almond milk, grated zucchini, vanilla extract, and optional cinnamon to the mug. Mix well until smooth and combined.

3. Microwave on high for about 60-90 seconds, or until the bread is cooked through and firm.

4. Let the zucchini bread cool for a minute before enjoying.

**Average Preparation Time**: 5 minutes

## 39. Keto Mug Sausage Gravy:

### Ingredients:
- 2 tablespoons cooked and crumbled sausage
- 2 tablespoons heavy cream
- 1 tablespoon cream cheese
- Pinch of garlic powder
- Pinch of onion powder
- Salt and pepper to taste

**Preparation:**

1. In a microwave-safe mug, combine the cooked and crumbled sausage, heavy cream, cream cheese, garlic powder, onion powder, salt, and pepper.

2. Microwave on high for about 1-2 minutes, stirring halfway through, until the sausage is heated through and the gravy is creamy.

3. Let the sausage gravy cool for a minute before serving.

**Average Preparation Time**: 5 minutes

# 40. Keto Mug Raspberry Cheesecake:

Ingredients:
- 2 tablespoons cream cheese
- 1 tablespoon heavy cream
- 1 tablespoon low-carb sweetener (such as stevia or erythritol)
- 1 tablespoon almond flour
- ¼ teaspoon vanilla extract
- 2-3 fresh raspberries

**Preparation:**

1. In a microwave-safe mug, whisk together the cream cheese, heavy cream, sweetener, almond flour, and vanilla extract until smooth and well combined.

2. Gently fold in the fresh raspberries.

3. Microwave on high for about 60-90 seconds, or until the cheesecake is set but still slightly soft in the center.

4. Let the raspberry cheesecake cool for a minute before enjoying.

**Average Preparation Time**: 5 minutes

## 41. Keto Mug Chicken Curry:

### Ingredients:
- 2 tablespoons cooked chicken, diced
- 2 tablespoons coconut milk
- 1 tablespoon tomato paste
- 1 tablespoon almond butter
- 1 teaspoon curry powder
- Pinch of garlic powder
- Pinch of onion powder
- Pinch of turmeric
- Salt and pepper to taste

### Preparation:

1. In a microwave-safe mug, combine the diced cooked chicken, coconut milk, tomato paste, almond butter, curry powder, garlic powder, onion powder, turmeric, salt, and pepper.

2. Microwave on high for about 1-2 minutes, stirring halfway through, until the chicken curry is heated through and the flavors are well combined.

3. Let the chicken curry cool for a minute before serving. Optional: Garnish with fresh cilantro.

**Average Preparation Time**: 5 minutes

## 42. Keto Mug Almond Flour Cookie:

### Ingredients:
- 2 tablespoons almond flour
- 1 tablespoon low-carb sweetener (such as stevia or erythritol)
- 1 tablespoon melted butter
- ¼ teaspoon vanilla extract
- Pinch of salt

**Preparation**:

1. In a microwave-safe mug, whisk together the almond flour, sweetener, melted butter, vanilla extract, and salt until well combined.

2. Microwave on high for about 60-90 seconds, or until the cookie is golden and cooked through.

3. Let the almond flour cookie cool for a minute before enjoying.

**Average Preparation Time**: 5 minutes

## 43. Keto Mug Sloppy Joe:

### Ingredients:
- 2 tablespoons ground beef or turkey
- 1 tablespoon low-carb tomato sauce
- 1 tablespoon diced onion
- 1 tablespoon diced bell pepper
- ½ teaspoon Worcestershire sauce
- Pinch of garlic powder
- Pinch of onion powder
- Salt and pepper to taste

**Preparation:**

1. In a microwave-safe mug, cook the ground beef or turkey until browned.

2. Drain any excess fat and add the tomato sauce, diced onion, diced bell pepper, Worcestershire sauce, garlic powder, onion powder, salt, and pepper to the mug.

3. Microwave on high for about 2-3 minutes, or until the mixture is heated through.

4. Stir the Sloppy Joe well to combine all the ingredients.

5. Let it cool for a minute before enjoying.

**Average Preparation Time**: 5 minutes

## 44. Keto Mug Apple Crisp:

### Ingredients:
- ½ small apple, peeled and diced
- 2 tablespoons almond flour
- 1 tablespoon low-carb sweetener (such as stevia or erythritol)
- 1 tablespoon melted butter
- ½ teaspoon cinnamon
- Pinch of nutmeg
- Pinch of salt

### Preparation:

1. In a microwave-safe mug, combine the diced apple, almond flour, sweetener, melted butter, cinnamon, nutmeg, and salt.

2. Microwave on high for about 2-3 minutes, or until the apple is tender.

3. Stir the apple crisp well to combine all the ingredients.

4. Let it cool for a minute before enjoying. Optional: Top with whipped cream or a sprinkle of additional cinnamon.

**Average Preparation Time**: 5 minutes

# 45. Keto Mug Meatloaf:

**Ingredients**:
- 2 tablespoons ground beef or turkey
- 1 tablespoon almond flour
- 1 tablespoon grated Parmesan cheese
- 1 tablespoon low-carb ketchup
- 1 tablespoon diced onion
- 1 teaspoon Worcestershire sauce
- Pinch of garlic powder
- Pinch of onion powder
- Salt and pepper to taste

**Preparation:**

1. In a microwave-safe mug, combine the ground beef or turkey, almond flour, Parmesan cheese, ketchup, diced onion, Worcestershire sauce, garlic powder, onion powder, salt, and pepper.

2. Mix well until all the ingredients are thoroughly combined.

3. Microwave on high for about 2-3 minutes, or until the meatloaf is cooked through.

4. Let the meatloaf cool for a minute before enjoying.

**Average Preparation Time**: 5 minutes

# 46. Keto Mug Key Lime Pie:

**Ingredients:**
- 2 tablespoons cream cheese
- 1 tablespoon heavy cream
- 1 tablespoon low-carb sweetener (such as stevia or erythritol)
- 1 tablespoon fresh lime juice
- ½ teaspoon lime zest
- Pinch of vanilla extract

**Preparation:**

1. In a microwave-safe mug, whisk together the cream cheese, heavy cream, sweetener, lime juice, lime zest, and vanilla extract until smooth and well combined.

2. Microwave on high for about 60-90 seconds, or until the key lime pie is set.

3. Let the key lime pie cool for a minute before enjoying.

**Average Preparation Time**: 5 minutes

## 47. Keto Mug Teriyaki Chicken:

**Ingredients:**
- 2 tablespoons diced chicken breast
- 1 tablespoon soy sauce (or coconut aminos for a soy-free option)
- 1 tablespoon water
- 1 tablespoon low-carb sweetener (such as stevia or erythritol)
- ½ teaspoon sesame oil
- Pinch of garlic powder
- Pinch of ginger powder

**Preparation:**

1. In a microwave-safe mug, combine the diced chicken breast, soy sauce, water, sweetener, sesame oil, garlic powder, and ginger powder.

2. Microwave on high for about 2-3 minutes, or until the chicken is cooked through.

3. Stir the teriyaki chicken well to coat it in the sauce.

4. Let it cool for a minute before serving. Optional: Garnish with sliced green onions and sesame seeds.

**Average Preparation Time**: 5 minutes

## 48. Keto Mug Pesto Cauliflower Rice:

### Ingredients:

- ½ cup cauliflower rice

- 2 tablespoons prepared pesto sauce

- 1 tablespoon grated Parmesan cheese

- Pinch of garlic powder

- Salt and pepper to taste

### Preparation:

1. In a microwave-safe mug, combine the cauliflower rice, pesto sauce, Parmesan cheese, garlic powder, salt, and pepper.

2. Microwave on high for about 2-3 minutes, or until the cauliflower rice is tender.

3. Stir the pesto cauliflower rice well to combine all the flavors.

4. Let it cool for a minute before enjoying.

**Average Preparation Time**: 5 minutes

## 49. Keto Mug Snickerdoodle Cookie:

### Ingredients:
- 2 tablespoons almond flour
- 1 tablespoon low-carb sweetener (such as stevia or erythritol)
- 1 tablespoon melted butter
- ¼ teaspoon vanilla extract
- ¼ teaspoon cinnamon
- Pinch of salt

### Preparation:

1. In a microwave-safe mug, whisk together the almond flour, sweetener, melted butter, vanilla extract, cinnamon, and salt until well combined.

2. Microwave on high for about 60-90 seconds, or until the cookie is golden and cooked through.

3. Let the snickerdoodle cookie cool for a minute before enjoying.

**Average Preparation Time**: 5 minutes

# 50. Keto Mug Beef and Broccoli Stir-Fry:

## Ingredients:
- 2 tablespoons cooked beef, sliced
- 2 tablespoons broccoli florets
- 1 tablespoon soy sauce
(or coconut aminos for a soy-free option)
- 1 tablespoon water
- Pinch of garlic powder
- Pinch of ginger powder
- Salt and pepper to taste

## Preparation:

1. In a microwave-safe mug, combine the sliced cooked beef, broccoli florets, soy sauce, water, garlic powder, ginger powder, salt, and pepper.

2. Microwave on high for about 2-3 minutes, or until the beef and broccoli are heated through.

3. Stir the beef and broccoli well to coat them in the sauce.

4. Let it cool for a minute before serving.

**Average Preparation Time**: 5 minutes

# Tips for Success and Troubleshooting

When making mug recipes, there are a few common issues that people may encounter. Here are some of them along with tips to overcome them:

**1. Uneven Cooking:** Sometimes, the ingredients in a mug recipe may not cook evenly, resulting in overcooked or undercooked portions. To prevent this, ensure that you mix the ingredients well and distribute them evenly in the mug. You can also try stirring the mixture once or twice during the cooking process to promote even cooking.

**2. Dry Texture:** Mug recipes can sometimes turn out dry due to overcooking or using too little liquid. To avoid this, be mindful of the cooking time and adjust it based on the wattage of your microwave. Additionally, consider adding a tablespoon or two of liquid such as water, milk, or oil to the recipe to keep it moist.

**3. Overflowing:** Certain mug recipes, especially those with leavening agents like baking powder, may overflow during the cooking process. To prevent this, ensure that your mug is large enough to accommodate the mixture without overflowing. You can also place a microwave-safe plate or paper towel under the mug to catch any potential spills.

**4. Undercooked Center**: Sometimes, the center of a mug recipe may remain undercooked while the edges are done. To address this issue, try reducing the power level on your microwave to allow for more even cooking. Additionally, you can increase the cooking time in small increments until the center is fully cooked.

**5. Rubberiness**: Overcooking can lead to a rubbery texture in mug recipes. It's important to follow the suggested cooking time and adjust it as needed based on your microwave's power. Start with the recommended time and check for doneness before deciding whether to cook it further.

**6. Lack of Flavor**: Mug recipes can occasionally lack flavor due to the limited ingredients used. To enhance the taste, consider adding herbs, spices, extracts, or low-carb sweeteners to the recipe. Experiment with different flavor combinations to find what works best for you.

**7. Mugs Getting Hot**: Microwaving mugs can make them hot to touch, so it's important to handle them with caution. Use oven mitts or a kitchen towel when removing the mug from the microwave to avoid burns. Let it cool for a short while before handling or consuming the contents.

# Tips to achieve the perfect mug dish every time

To achieve the perfect mug dish every time, here are some helpful tips:

**1. Use the Right Size Mug**: Ensure that you're using an appropriately sized mug for the recipe. The mug should have enough capacity to accommodate the ingredients without overflowing during cooking.

**2. Mix Ingredients Thoroughly**: Take the time to mix the ingredients well, ensuring that all the components are evenly distributed. This helps to ensure consistent flavor and texture throughout the dish.

**3. Adjust Cooking Time and Power:** Microwave wattages can vary, so it's important to adjust the cooking time and power level accordingly. Start with the recommended cooking time in the recipe, but be prepared to make adjustments based on your microwave's power. If your microwave tends to cook things quickly, reduce the cooking time slightly. If it cooks slowly, increase the cooking time accordingly.

**4. Pause and Stir**: If you notice uneven cooking or hot spots during the cooking process, pause the microwave and give the mixture a stir. This helps to distribute heat and promotes even cooking.

**5. Check for Doneness**: Always check the doneness of your mug dish before assuming it's fully cooked. Insert a toothpick or a small knife into the center of the dish, and if it comes out clean or with minimal crumbs, it's usually done. If it's not fully cooked, return it to the microwave for additional cooking time in short increments.

**6. Resting Time**: Allow your mug dish to rest for a minute or two after removing it from the microwave. This allows the heat to distribute evenly and helps to set the dish, improving its texture and flavor.

**7. Customize to Taste**: Feel free to customize the recipe to suit your preferences. Adjust the seasoning, add extra ingredients, or incorporate toppings to enhance the flavor and make it your own.

**8. Experiment and Have Fun:** Don't be afraid to experiment with different flavors, ingredients, and cooking techniques. Mug recipes offer a lot of flexibility and room for creativity, so have fun exploring new combinations and variations.

Remember, practice makes perfect. Don't get discouraged if your first attempt doesn't turn out exactly as expected. With some trial and error, you'll soon become a pro at creating delicious mug dishes.

# CONCLUSION

Congratulations! You've reached the end of this keto mug recipe book, and we hope it has been a source of inspiration, convenience, and deliciousness on your ketogenic journey. The world of mug cooking has opened up a whole new realm of possibilities, proving that healthy, low-carb meals can be effortlessly prepared in a matter of minutes.

Throughout this book, we've explored a wide range of flavors, textures, and culinary creations that showcase the versatility of mug recipes. From indulgent breakfasts to satisfying main courses and decadent desserts, each recipe has been meticulously designed to adhere to the principles of the ketogenic diet while delivering exceptional taste.

We hope that these recipes have sparked your imagination and encouraged you to experiment with your own variations and personal touches. The simplicity of mug cooking allows for endless customization, enabling you to tailor each recipe to your unique preferences and dietary needs.

Remember, the journey to a healthier lifestyle is a continuous one, and embracing the ketogenic diet is a step in the right direction. By incorporating these keto mug recipes into your daily routine, you've taken control of your nutrition without sacrificing flavor or convenience.

As you move forward, we encourage you to continue exploring the world of keto cooking, expanding your culinary repertoire and embracing new challenges. The principles you've learned from this book—portion control, mindful ingredient selection, and the power of creativity—will serve as valuable tools in your ongoing quest for health and well-being.

We sincerely hope that this book has empowered you to embark on a lifelong culinary adventure, where the combination of keto principles and the simplicity of mug cooking become the foundation of your healthy eating habits. May your mugs be filled with nourishing and delicious creations that fuel your body and bring joy to your taste buds.

Thank you for joining us on this delicious journey, and here's to a future filled with flavorful, convenient, and keto-friendly mug recipes. Cheers!

Made in the USA
Middletown, DE
25 October 2024

63252860R00046